Top of Mind

Discovering some things we already know

Value
Ethics
Strength
True *(being true)*

. . . .

From the notebooks of:

Dominic Wharram

Dominic Wharram

ISBN: 978-1507550311 (paperback)

Also available as an ebook.

Copies of *Top of Mind* are available at special discounts for bulk purchases by corporations, institutions and other organizations.

For more information contact:
Dominic Wharram by visiting Dcoached.com

*The **W Select** logo on this book means a significant portion of the proceeds is being donated to a charity. Visit dCoached.com for more details.*

THANK YOU

Clearly there are too many people to thank for allowing me to draw upon my experience with them. So I will remain indebted to many. A few, however, helped get this into an actual book:

Phillip, for giving this stuff a name and for an honest opinion along the way.

Glenn for thinking long and hard. Invaluable.

Paul - a man with whom I have never had any business — yet we work well together and I am grateful.

Kate - I know punctuation matters. I just can't seem to do it properly ... Thank you.

Walter and Phil ... You are to blame for all this ya know. Thank you for asking.

And Linda - You are awesome. Always have been even when I didn't know it.

Notes …

CONTENTS

Notes …

QUICK INTRODUCTION …

When I work with small groups or individuals on the topics here in this book I have had generally two kinds of responses and then an interesting follow up. One of the response types is along the lines of "This is stuff I already know. Thank you for bringing it top of mind." Incidentally, that's a real quote and so I used it to name the book (Thank you, Phillip). The other type of response is some variation of: "So simple. We all know this stuff … how is it that we lose it along the way?"

Hearing those kind of remarks over and over early on made me think: "…well, maybe this stuff isn't that important if everyone knows it". But then the interesting follow-up has been referrals and invitations and introductions to others to share it some more.

I guess when I think of what I have been doing for the past 25 years, it boils down to my quietly helping good folks succeed for the most part. Along that path I have seen some devastating failures of people, both good folks and those hell bent on some sort of ultimate destruction it seemed (including family and friends). And I have seen some wonderful success for people, both the kind of folks who planned it all out and those to whom it happened by accident. The thing ALL of them had in common is what I have tried to capture in this book.

They all knew the topics covered in this book. Some had a way to keep this type of information top of mind in their lives and found ways to make it part of their daily lives. The others wish they had. They all knew these concepts to be fundamentals no matter what.

So - for those of you into spoilers, here's what's in store with the rest of this book.
- There is nothing new in this book. You and I already know all this stuff. Most people do in fact. Even those that have spectacular failures or personal regrets can look at what's in this book and say, "Yep, I know. I just didn't do anything about any of it."
- This stuff is easy … and yet we still benefit from reminders once in a while because other things distract us. This book is one of those reminders for us.
- And finally, this book provides a few concrete tricks that can help put these fundamental concepts all Top of Mind again so we can keep them there every day of our lives, in every instance and with every interaction.

I've also been told by folks this stuff changes lives. I hope that's ok with you.

Notes ...

Notes …

Top of Mind

First - A quick story:

> **Note:** Even though the story has a business setting, stick with it because I believe it is relatable to just about everyone.

I'm a lucky guy. I had the opportunity to chat with a number of business executives candidly about what makes things work and what things gum up the works no matter the industry. It was a great conversation! I also had the rare opportunity to pose an off the cuff question to this cross section of business leaders. I'm lucky because the question I posed they actually found interesting and they were willing to answer it!

I simply asked the group: "What is the upper most top of mind business word that defines your day more often than not?" Almost simultaneously a number of responses came and some smirks and some laughter and all without any further prompting. It was just that easy for anyone to answer and keep answering as they played off the others answers from others in the group. I wrote it all down on the whiteboard in the room. I made a PowerPoint slide years ago with those words on it and I share it a little later on. But I have to finish the story first.

The laughter ended and they all looked at me as if I had a point to the question or a witty remark or something. I had nothing. I just had the opportunity to ask the question so I took it without really thinking.

So I punted. I started to speak some words out of a mild panic. I really am a lucky guy because the words caught their attention. I asked the same question but made it personal since the first one was all business.

> *"What is the upper most top of mind word for your **personal life** that defines your day apart from work and the office more often than not?"*

This time, however, they were slow to respond and silent at first. Since I didn't know I was going to ask that question I didn't really have a clue how to prompt the conversation along so the room sat silent for a bit, but I will add that it wasn't uncomfortable. The question struck a cord and people were thinking. The silence was that very specific sound of thought happening in the room.

That was the beginning of me culling my notes around the VEST. I began to compile my notes and thoughts around my professional experience in various industries working with professionals at all levels of organizations. **Value**, **Ethics**, **Strength** and **True** became the four major themes that emerged. They seemed to be the roots as I learned the power of self reflection and future impact. Fortunately I have the real honor to call friends some very cool people in all walks of life and at all levels of various businesses and organizations. I draw on that experience for examples of what's good and what's bad. Much of it boils down to the four topics we cover in this book as the simple foundation for what I have witnessed as a sound life. My hope is that it makes sense to you personally as we cover each of the topics, not just from some sort of distant way when you see how it applied to someone else from whom I may draw on for examples, but personally as you start to think of how this applies to your daily life. We will see how it goes here for you.

I will do my best to illustrate things with experiences for us so that the things we talk about over the course of this book stick in ways that are personal for you rather than just sets of words I string together.

Here's the exercise I do with small groups and individuals when we are talking about things that are 'top of mind'. As I shared above, this is how it all began when I was working with that group of business folks. Grab a pencil ... pen ... crayon because we are about to dive into a personal experience.

Answer this question with two or three separate words:

What is top of mind for you right now?

```
Answer here:



```

Anyone can answer this question. It's really open ended, but given the context of our day and what we do during our day and how people know us, two or three words usually bubble up pretty quickly. And sometimes there are so many variables that it's hard to pick a line of thought personally to begin the process of choosing three words. Note that the time of day and where we are physically as well as what's going on emotionally for us all impact the possible answers at the moment the question is asked. For example, if I am talking to someone in the clergy, they will generally have 'God' or 'prayer' in the top 1-5 words and it may not matter what else is going on in their life or the time of day. Or Day Care providers, no matter what time of day or where they are or what's going on, will have 'children' near the top. Teachers have 'students or kids' top of mind pretty much all the time.

Here's that PowerPoint I built years ago demonstrating what a group of business people had on their mind when I asked them:

So teachers have their list, the clergy have theirs, business professionals have their words — I have my words and you have yours. And given the context of our lives, our lists may change depending on when we come up with the words.

Think of the lists the various type of people I mentioned might come up with. Or maybe think of the list of words various people in your life might come up with. Reflect on your list perhaps. All are pretty good lists aren't they? But if you and I had a chance to talk about your list as I do with with friends in groups about their collection of words making up their lists, we realize that given the context of why you think of different words is almost endless and all of them are influenced by something that we all have in common actually. We will get to it — but let's carry on for a moment.

Consider another list for a moment; for the most part, all of us have people around us in our lives.

We have-
- *Co workers*
- *Family*
- *Friends*
- *Perhaps a spouse or significant other*
- *Maybe children*

You have probably already started to think of specific people or groups of folks in your life once you started reading the list there.

So given the circumstances of life and our day, the people around us that we either influence or who influence us, all impact what really is top of mind at any given time. And that's what this book is all about.

What really is top of mind and why it is top of mind. So, it's true, this isn't the sort of book where I share some secret ways to move mountains, and I don't try and introduce something 'new' and 'exciting' that I know and wish to impart to the world as a superior way to think/do something. What I try to do is reconcile an interesting part of our lives common to all of us.

I like to look at it this way:

Everyone that influences your life AND everyone whose life you influence have something in common. Every word and every emotion and every thought that crosses your mind in every interaction with people, have something in common.

YOU

You are at the center of all of it. I'm not talking about the ego-maniacal center of the universe, the world revolves around me, type thinking. I'm talking about our personal sphere of influence. The kind of influence where we are influenced by others. And the kind where we have an influence on or over others. The words that come top of mind shift a bit from time to time based on shifts in people, circumstances, time of day and physical location just to name a few factors — all parts of our sphere of influence.

The notes I culled for this conversation landing on these four major themes span over the past 25 years; I have done no scientific research into anything I'm sharing in this book. What I am sharing has come from my work with people in several industries at all levels of business interaction as well as my personal life including my family and friends. Over the course of my career I have learned/observed a few things that all of us will probably recognize:

- People (that includes you and me) want good things. Some want good things for themselves. Some want good things for others and some want both with varying degrees of which takes precedence .
- We all want less bad things to happen to ourselves or others
- **And the happiest, most positively impactful and personally successful people with whom I have worked all have mastered four things.**

Now I know that last point is a bit wordy – My wife even pointed it out to me as 'too wordy'. I couldn't cut the words down any (Or I'm not talented enough a writer to cut them down). They will become a theme of sorts that we will revisit from time to time in subsequent pages. It's key to why the four sections of this book exist. So they are stuck in my head this way.

What I do in this book is recount my notes in those four big buckets as reminders for us. I used the word 'reminders' because they are things THAT WE ALREADY KNOW. The goal then is to have them remain top of mind.

I have also put some critical thought into how we can put this stuff to work in our life, simply, consistently and easily from now on without allowing distraction to take them away from us ever again. The folks who I can think of across my career and in my personal life that have mastered these fundamentals seem to make it all so easy. So, I have simplified each of the four things into simple tools so we can have them REMAIN top of mind for the rest of our life too.

We already know the words, and there is a 'chapter' dedicated to each:

VALUE   ETHICS   STRENGTH   TRUE

The way we explore the meaning of each word above may be a little different than you might be immediately thinking about them. But at the end of this quick read, you will be saying to yourself that I have read your mind and this is all stuff you do indeed already know.

Notes ...

VALUE

Remember how I said I like to illustrate things with experiences? Let's try another one now:

Maybe you remember the childhood game "What are you?" It's a harmless little game a group of children play where the question to everyone is "What are you?" It starts off with the predictable answers:

Brother, Son, Daughter, Sister ...

Those are the easy answers. All of us are one of those, so it's an easy game to get going in the first place.

And then the answers turn into the exotic that may spark some conversations among young people:

Uncle, Aunt, Step Sister, Adopted ...

Think about those answers for a group of young kids. Someone who is eight that is an Aunt? Adopted? That spawns a whole slew of questions as you can imagine like, "Do you know your real parents ..." and maybe that question starts another conversation around what insensitive might mean — and on and on it might go. Can you see it? Do you remember playing?

And maybe the answers turn into something very interesting or provocative:

Surfer, Artist, Atheist …

What? Atheist? Really? Or maybe someone else is an artist too but never said it aloud, but they are bold enough to say it now and the conversation is about different kinds of artists. Can you see this game playing out? Did you play it as a kid? Are you secretly making a list in your head right now?

The game usually ends in some tangent conversation(s) around one of the interesting or provocative answers — and that might have been the point of the game being invented in the first place. I don't know. If nothing interesting or provocative pops up, then the answers turn into the ridiculous:

lawn-mower, dish-washer, class-clown, etc.

And then the answers just spiral into made-up new notions that the kids concoct around things they do, like cow-milker, diaper-changer, etc.

All the answers other than those that turned ridiculous had a pretty important theme. They address relationships. Did you catch that? As you secretly played it in your own head, were some of your answers along the lines of relationships? Playing the game, I can't help but envision people in my life and my answer describing my role in theirs.

Let's formalize this. let's play the game for real:

What are you?

Answer here (write as many things as you can in tiny little handwriting to get as many as you can in this box):

The childhood version of the question, however, isn't quite right for the importance of the topic. It should read "WHO are you?" The difference between "WHAT" and "WHO" is important to think about for a moment. If the answer to "WHAT am I?" is 'Uncle'; that's the end of it. I answered the question. Done. If the question is "WHO am I?" and my answer is 'Uncle,' then I have to finish the answer with a name of someone.

WHO am I?
I am an Uncle to Jenny, Josh and … etc. And so the answers to this game start to take on some real meaning

around the things in this world that are important. Relationships.

Kids get it, though. They aren't interested in the whole story. They ask WHAT so they can quickly get to something interesting or provocative without all the details and deep thinking. They want it to be fun and exciting. I, of course, want this to be dull and boring. That's not true, but in groups (as opposed to reading it in a book) we can have some fun going off the rails for a bit talking about something exciting someone might come up with.

I have to share this quick story with you. A very funny answer that someone gave in a group setting was 'Mega-rock-star'. He said it out loud — and seriously. This stumped everyone since everyone worked with him. He was not a rock-star, certainly not a mega-rock-star. He was the head of a Systems Analyst group. I thought maybe we just learned something we didn't know about someone in the group, so I asked him about it. We did in fact learn something new. This guy was actually very funny and we didn't know that about him (in fact, I learned that people regarded him as very serious, along the lines of a stick-in-the-mud kind of fun guy). However, we learned that his humor was a great addition for all of the rest of the morning that we spent together. His answer when I asked him about his super cool and very exciting answer was, "I included my dreams for this game". I actually just laughed out loud in my office typing this as I recalled the scenario! So he was answering who he was in his dreams. Cool. Funny.

Getting back on track here, we need to think about the details behind our answers for just a moment while we are on the topic of VALUE.

Most of us have a list of who we are to or with others that include personal answers:

> **Mother, Father, Uncle, Aunt, Brother, Spouse, Friend …**

And then we may have answers around our positions with regard to groups:

> **Boss, Team Mate, Colleague, Friend …**

And then we may have actual titles in our list:

> **Teacher, Rabbi, CEO, Vice President, Pastor, Operations Manager, Lead Systems Analyst …**

All are right answers, of course. Those groupings above may prove helpful to you as you think about your answers. So, think of your answers in terms of the context in which you live your life and how relationships impact your life and how you impact the lives of others.

Remember that we are talking about VALUE in this section and the trick here will be for us to think about VALUE and how that relates to the people in our life in those three main areas:

> ***Personally*** *(family and friends)*

Within groups *(Hobbies, clubs and work groups)*
and Professionally *(Your title — what you do)*

Just as we noted in the quick intro that everyone wants more good stuff and less bad stuff. It's true in every relationship too. The calculation of good and bad is what drives VALUE. But it's tricky and yet simple:

Let's consider a single financial transaction somewhere during our day:

We need Coffee. *(Sidebar here. We don't actually need coffee. I'm using this as an example since in my case I really do need coffee to satisfy a small addiction I have in which case I get a headache if I don't get it).* I digress. We need coffee and they will want money in exchange for it. So will the exchange be a GOOD value or a BAD value? The price is $2.24 for my cup of coffee or $11.99 for a bag of whole beans for the expensive brand or 7.99 for the house brand.   Making the purchase or not making the purchase, or which purchase I make all says something about what I consider the best value. Time of day, who I am with, how bad/good things are going that day all play into the decision.

These are evaluations we make everyday about money and everything on which we spend it. Maybe we do this with time as well? I may forego one meeting and opt for another. This is the time well spent versus a waste of time example.   **But how does this relate to relationships?**

Here is that theme of sorts that we had a look at in the

quick intro:

The happiest, most positively impactful and personally successful people all have mastered four things.

VALUE is one of the four things they have mastered and it is in regard specifically to EVERY relationship they have both personally and professionally. But there is a catch to understanding how they do it. None of them ask themselves "How will I evaluate the value of my relationships as it relates to Dom's game of Who am I?" They don't think in terms of exchanging one thing for another (like money for coffee). And they seldom if ever think of what's in it for them given which meeting to attend in lieu of another at the same time. They do something far more profound. So when I gave that example of money for coffee and asked how that relates to Value when it comes to relationships? The answer is:

> **It doesn't work like that for relationships. Not with those folks who are the happiest, most impactful and personally successful.**

They know WHO they are today just like you do in terms of the relationships in your list from the game. They have their list, too, regardless of if they write it down or not like we did.

They didn't find a magical calculation to determine the value of each relationship. Instead they have turned the concept into   a   far   more   successful   method   of calculating it. They have figured out a way to make the calculation always work for them AND the other person/group/team, consistent, In fact, with EVERY interaction.

The answer for them is a personal resolve.

They have resolved to <u>provide</u> VALUE in EVERY interaction.

They resolved to provide value. It's a way of life for them. It's the way they roll. It's how they do things. It's how they are. Period. Simple, right? This means that they are going to do everything in their power to make sure the value of the interaction is known and felt and realized by the other person (or group or team etc.). They are giving — and the old question of what's in it for them? Well … just that. The knowledge that they had just done what they can to provide value to and or for someone else. Think about that. It's pretty powerful and you know it when you see it in others. You are likely thinking of people in your life who fit that description. You might even be thinking about where and to whom you do this (or should be this in their lives). These people don't think of what meeting is best for them when they have to choose. They figure out where they will be most useful to the others in the meeting and go to that one. It's subtle and extremely powerful stuff.

So this is easy, right? The concept is simple for sure. And for anyone to master anything, they have to do it. And then they have to do it consistently. As a normal way of 'being'; eventually, it just becomes part of who they are and ultimately recognized for it. It's a characteristic that just 'is' and it's hard to point to IT as the thing that is underlying their positive impact on others. But when you see it, you know it. And when it's you, it's likely because you have simply resolved to be that way. It's magic.

What I love about it is that we know this down deep. We just may have not developed a habit around it. Maybe some of those other top of mind words overshadow it or push it out of mind every once in a while. And maybe it gets pushed aside for a few days in a row — then weeks, then months — then it really only pops up once in a while. But it's still in there for all of us.

So there is a simple tool we can put in our personal toolbox. But before we talk about the specific tool, I want to make sure we are not oversimplifying something pretty important.

Let's consider that theme of sorts for our discussion:

> **The _happiest_, most _positively impactful_ and _personally successful_ people all have mastered four things.**

There are three things in that description, that in my opinion and in my experience, describe someone I hope everyone has the privilege to know someday. Heck. I aspire to be that kind of person one day. People like that are truly inspirational and not necessarily in a motivational speaker kind of way. When you know them, you know it about them. Check out the

23

underlined words above.

Happy doesn't mean 'bubbly' or 'perky'. It means **confident** and **grateful** in this context.

Positively impactful doesn't mean having 'influence' or 'power'. It means **humble** and **exemplary** here.

Personally successful doesn't have much if anything to do with 'wealth' or 'social status'. It has everything to do with being **accomplished** and **willing and comfortable with that**.

Think of the immense contrast that the meaning of the words can bring to our attention:

Would we rather spend an hour with someone who is:

Confident and grateful, humble and exemplary, accomplished, willing and comfortable being ... with you.

Or someone who is:

Bubbly and perky, influential and powerful, wealthy and famous ... in the publics eye.

Although it's easy to spot individuals in the news of the latter sort, and it is pretty cool to meet one from time to time from a novelty standpoint, I think most of us honestly want to get on in life and have a few of the first type around us more often than not. Which do you aspire to be, to your son or daughter or to anyone else on the list of folks you wrote down in the game of WHO are you?

This is NOT a judgment call around what and who is good or bad. This has to do with the reality of who we are in life. Who we are to and with the people in our life and what it takes to be the best at bringing the most good in that world we call our life.

This is about our consideration of what it takes in our life to:

Resolve to Provide VALUE.

I have two quick stories for us that help me keep this in perspective:

"Beer in the fridge story"

I was doing some work for an executive leadership team all of whom reported to a CEO. I had a 40-second interaction with that CEO by happen-chance, late one afternoon, about some beer in the little conference room fridge. She let me know to leave it alone if I were looking for something to drink. It was a lighthearted conversation all in good fun. We had made eye contact and we did exchange our names - 40 seconds tops. Fully three years later passing one another in a completely difference building and setting and again by happen-chance I said, "Hello, Ms. SoandSo *(not her real name)"*. Once we made eye contact she replied, "Hi Dominic, how good it is to run into you. I hope things are going well?" and stopping to chat, she made what could have been a passing hello an engaging question. We caught up professionally for about a minute and a half. As I have recounted this story with others who know her, they are not surprised at all. They all have similar stories and so, we now have an example of someone who actively commits to providing value.

My guess is that you can think of at least one person who is that kind of person. If you can, think now what made that person come to mind? There's a quality there that you just know and feel, isn't there? That's the thing. When you experience it or see it in another person, they have mastered the concept of VALUE that we are covering here. They simply have built a habit around it and it's part of who they are. What's even cooler is that we can all do this, everyday, FROM NOW ON!

Let me share another quick one before we move on:

"The gracious boss story"
Working with an operational team on some restructuring of processes, we prepared the updates the leader was going to share with the COO (his boss). We had a tight schedule, limited time and the COO had a real desire for his operational leaders to be succinct. The leader presenting to the COO with a majority of his team in attendance was on the verge of faltering a bit once he realized that the time was running short and he wouldn't be able to complete the presentation.

Before he could have a second chance to allow his worry to enter his voice, the COO interrupted very thoughtfully and suggested three things to reset the meeting. First, that everything so far was excellently prepared and thoughtful and exactly on target (he removed any fears from the leader in continuing). Second, he mentioned that the time would not allow the leader to do justice to the rest of the presentation and suggested that we complete the current and next point, and schedule a second meeting to complete the agenda fully — no altering of it (removed the anxiety of time constraints). Thirdly he noted the richness of the content was an example for everyone listening for future updates and statuses given the complexity of the work and the expertise of the teams doing this work, (established buy-in for everyone on the call).

I like to think that this example shows the COO listening first and asking what he can learn. AND then when given the time to speak he clearly asked himself how he can help. I think that type of listening and response is a gift. It's one worth noting because it is the secret to what VALUE is in any relationship.

So let's get to it. What's the secret? What's the magic?

There really is only one way to resolve to provide value in every single interaction with any person for the rest of your life.

Ask yourself these two questions early and often in every situation where you are interacting with someone else. After a while, they too will be either a habit, or just part of who you are:

If we are the first one to talk, the question to ask ourselves in our head:

"How can I help?"

If we are listening first, the question to ask ourselves in our head:

"What can I learn?"

<u>Let's consider "How can I help"</u>:
When we talk we tend to want to be heard. We tend to focus on our voice. We tend to think about how the person listening to us will think about how we sound.

If we go into that next interaction with whomever it is asking **"how can I help?",** chances are we will end up asking more questions and learning more and listening more than we ever dreamed. As I began to practice this I found myself interested to learn more about <u>active listening</u> which deepened my understanding of listening beyond just my preparation to respond. This changed my life and it may change your life as well to read up on the science behind active listening. Asking that simple little question of ourselves will change everything and the people around us will notice the change right from the start. Putting this in motion sets yourself apart just like the examples you were thinking of just a moment ago. It's something special and now it's for all of us.

Then when you can actually help, what you impart, how you impart it, why you chose exactly what you intend to impart, will be received with the value the other can truly count on from you FROM NOW ON. And the added value that can't be calculated? They came to you in the first place for a reason. You met it and exceeded it. It's now who you are. Is it worth it?

Let's consider "What can I learn":
When we listen we tend to hear breaks in the conversation and take that as a cue that it's our turn to talk. We tend to sense a question in the way they speak, so we prepare responses or examples. We tend to tune out topics where we think we have experience or knowledge because we think we won't learn anything new from whoever is talking.

If we listen and ask ourselves **"What can I learn?"**, chances are we will end up truly learning and wanting to learn more which will lead to a conversation and the relationship can only grow from there.

Then, once you've listened fully, the two of you (you and the group/team, etc., whatever) will have something more in common for sure footing ready to discuss anything for greater results, even if those results are nothing more than a more rewarding relationship.

This is one of the four things a great leader/boss/spouse/brother/sister/aunt/uncle/friend masters and then makes part of their life forever more. My hope for you is that starting next week, this is part of your life. Just let those two questions roll around in the back of your head for the rest of your life … you too can master the resolve it takes to provide value in every relationship in which you find yourself.

This is the first secret power, the first bit of magic for the folks I am talking about when I say:

The happiest, most positively impactful and personally successful people all have mastered four things.

You time -

- OK, here we are at the end of the first section. If I'm working with a small group, I grab my ipad and play some music on my jambox so everyone can jot down a few notes. There is absolutely no fear that what you jot down will be shared with the group or with me or with anyone ... so enjoy the music and take some notes.

The next page is a close representation of the 3"x5" card I hand out and the idea is to simply put some thoughtful checkmarks where it applies to your life.

The idea has us consider "Who we are" ... and how we might take our new tools from this section to those people in our life. If it applies, go ahead and make a check mark. If it doesn't – skip it.

This simple exercise has us start to actually think about those two questions as they might apply to our relationship with real people in our life ... starting with the very next interaction.

Crank the tunes ... grab a cup of coffee ... whatever it takes for you to be thoughtful for a minute about how this applies to your life.

For this card, place some check marks where you will actively think of the VALUE questions noted in this chapter towards the people listed, or as the person you are to others …

Value

Value - Ethics - Strengths - True

☐ Towards my   ☐ As a   **Dad**

☐ Towards my   ☐ As a   **Mom**

☐ Towards my   ☐ As a   **Brother**

☐ Towards my   ☐ As a   **Sister**

☐ Towards my   ☐ As an   **Aunt**

☐ Towards my   ☐ As an   **Uncle**

☐ Towards my   ☐ As a   **Friends**

☐ Towards my   ☐ As a   **Spouse**

☐ Towards my   ☐ As a   **Boss/Leader**

☐ Towards my   ☐ As a   **Child(ren)**

☐ Towards my   ☐ As an   **Employee(s)**

☐ Towards my   ☐ As a   **Neighbor**

☐ Towards my   ☐ As a   **Colleague(s)**

☐ Towards my   ☐ As a   _____

☐ Towards my   ☐ As a   _____

The point: The above people are important to you and you are important to them.
So ask yourself …

When Speaking: **How can I help?**
When Listening: **What can I learn?**

© D. Wharram. Top Of Mind. dCoached.com

Ethics

Goodness this is a big topic. In fact, it's a ginormous industry too. It's a topic that I think has become overly complex given what the core of it really is. It's about doing the right thing or doing it as often as possible and doing the wrong thing as little as possible, at a minimum. Unfortunately, that simple core of an idea has been lost somehow and our court systems and court of public opinion are filled with white collar crime, fraud, spectacular fails by sports figures, business moguls, religious leaders and pop culture icons. A stunning topic that doesn't touch the bulk of us quite like that ... or does it?

Lawyers write policies for companies and organizations that outline ethical guidelines by which company executives are to abide. Religious leaders share messages of faith that fall into categories of ethics often enough. Therapists deal with folks overcoming lapses in judgment often around ethical concerns. I'm not a lawyer. I am not ordained in any religion. I have no therapy clients. The topic of ETHICS is outside my credentials.

I'm going to tackle it anyway. The reason I'm tackling it is because you and I have some common ground when it comes to the topic of Ethics; We want good stuff more and bad stuff less. And both of us know things about good and bad, right and wrong — the gray area. Lies and truth, stealing, using others as well as caring and protecting; this stuff is not foreign to either of us and to consider the impact of all of them in our personal life doesn't require us to be lawyers, ordained or trained therapists. What is required is that we have a list of people in our lives, and we have that from the game we played earlier.

In my experience working with individuals, businesses and other organizations, risky business that skirts ethics has only two paths and both have the same outcome. It's this experience that addresses what the practical application of ethics looks like.

There is the path where we get away with 'it' and there is the path where we don't.

On the path where we get away with 'it', this does a couple things all by itself. One thing it can do is eat away at someone until it consumes them completely. The second thing it can do is become a catalyst for doing more of the same risky stuff. This path where we get away with 'it' is not a straight path. It's a spiral into hell itself for people. This path destroys people, business, reputations, marriages, friendships, relationships and lives … many many lives.

Now that other path. The path where we don't get away with 'it', as in — busted? It's the same pathway to hell, just quicker.

Redemption in either case is either far more costly than whatever the gain in the first place was, and that's the best case scenario I have ever seen. Worst case is there is no redemption or someone dies or both. And that's really as harsh as it sounds if that sounded too blunt. Consider our theme for the book:

The happiest, most positively impactful and personally successful people all have mastered four things.

These folks have a firm grasp on the impact of ETHICS in their life. They have a very specific guidepost and I would like to work through an example with you to help us understand this guidepost.

When I work with small groups, usually business professionals, we try to think of an example happening in the news. Honestly, I don't prepare one in advance and simply ask about someone recently or currently in the news that is a pretty good example of a stunning failure of something around ethics. The easy targets, usually on the front page, are Business moguls, pop-icons, religious leaders every once in a while and maybe a prominent politician.

As you are reading this today, can you think of an example in the news right now? Or has been recently that we can use?

Write the name of the person for this example:

Now given what this person has done or has allegedly done, can you think through what you would have done to make sure you wouldn't have gotten caught? You still had to do the thing they did (or allegedly did), but you think of how to do it better without getting caught.

Sidebar … Funny thing happened one day in a group I was working with. (*I'm sharing this quick story because I want to underscore the fact that I am not trying to illicit attempts at illegal activity with better planning.*) So … One guy in a group wanted to see if the group could come with a plan to embezzle money from a certain company. We all thought it was a little odd he brought that up as a hypothetical we should work on as a group instead of finding an example in the news to think through. I still half expect to see his name in the news one day for embezzlement.

Moving on …

Do you have your example? Did you write it in the box?

Can you research it enough or do you know enough about the situation to see what mistakes he/she made early on that led to getting caught?

Was it one mistake? For example, did you read about the guy who stole some things and left his Facebook page open at the house he robbed?

Was it many mistakes? For example, did you see the story of the guy who was a great pick pocket, but kept all the wallets and purses in his apartment which led to the selfie he posted showing all of them in the background prompting someone to investigate?

Was it a timing issue? Remember the fella working late at the 'office' when the spouse calls back to the office and it's closed?

Was the issue who was trusted was a mistake? Maybe you recall the mayor who buys crack from an agent posing as a street girl?

Maybe the issue is that the wrong people were involved right from the start? Like when the guy selling cocaine at his office teams up with the undercover FBI guy in the mail room for distribution.

Maybe it was lack of vision or short-sided planning? For example, in the news just the other day there was a get-away car in the plan and it was a brand new yellow Camaro. That should blend in just fine.

So what's the first issue you can fix with the scenario you chose? I encourage you to play it all the way through and see if you can solve the issue to be something that CAN be gotten away with if only they had used your solutions.

It's a very doable exercise, at least in terms of coming up with the better plan. Kinda fun in a twisted sort of way isn't it? This is just an exercise and if you are looking for a redeeming quality to this kind of twisted thinking apart from this exercise, here are two:

I have a friend who is a hired hacker. He's a good guy that has to think of how bad guys break through computer firewalls. He is paid to think this stuff through so others can plug those vulnerabilities. Another example was shortly after 9/11, I started thinking of how a bad guy could get bombs on planes and noticed a weakness at an airport that allowed for direct contact between secured areas and unsecured. I filed a report about it with the airport, I was never acknowledged, but that vulnerability was fixed within a couple weeks, I noticed. My guess is that a number of flyers pointed it out to the airport.

Back at it now ...

Once you have solved your riddle thinking it all the way through, continue on with the scenario and ask yourself what else needs to happen in your life now that you did 'it'. What lies do you need to manage? What changes in lifestyle need to occur? Which relationships need to be dealt with differently from now on for the rest of your life? Can you manage it? Will you be tempted to try another scary thing because you did it without getting caught this time? This is powerful stuff. Think how much energy you exerted planning it out and how much more it will take to manage it from now on. This is powerful stuff!

Remember that spiral I talked about earlier? Welcome to hell. And that was you getting away with 'it'? Now go read the story from the source where you got this example to read about the hell they are entering having gotten caught. This is the stuff happening everyday to people big and small … some hitting the news and most of them not hitting the news. I know that I have seen all kinds of people exert this kind of energy, some, for years. At the end of it all I can recall pondering, "If only they had exerted that energy into something good." You have probably asked yourself the same thing about examples you may know of.

The goal here is to make sure it's never you or me.

So let's talk about what we all know about ethics today.

Every Fortune 500 company has policies relating to ethics, proper conduct, staying within the bounds of the law, etc. A company with whom I do work does yearly background checks AND everyone, including contractors, signs documents stating they understand and will abide by the 'Code of Conduct' for the company. So if everyone is agreeing to abide by ethical codes of conduct, why does the company have to check up on employees and executives? Why do we have spectacular headlines? Every publicly traded company has training at some level for all the executives and some attestation to the effect that they will be good, yet these people go to jail all the time. And right now, there are countless others who are entering the spiral to hell because they have not yet been caught and they are covering their tracks.

We all say we know the difference between good and bad, yet prisons have all kinds of professionals who have crossed a line in business. There are individuals from all walks of faith who know the difference between good and bad yet we see them fall from grace all the time.

I know not every one is perfect, we are human. We all make mistakes, but think about some of these mistakes for a moment. When it comes to ethical issues and calculated risk we are crossing into a very difficult area to navigate. As far as temptations go, simple mistakes, these things do happen. But when we add plans and calculations to specifically not get caught, and think through plans and schemes to avoid being discovered, there is surly a line there that defines what we are talking about in this book and our lives.

It's that line that we are talking about. It's that kind of ETHICS we are addressing here. These things are sometimes very different from what the policy at work means or what the clergy might talk about or even the laws that govern our society.

There are two stark stories that demonstrate this concept. Both are extreme but on the opposite ends of each other.

There is the story of Ann Franke and the helpers who kept her family alive and in hiding during the occupation of Amsterdam in 1942. The laws of the land at the time provided for the Death Penalty for sheltering a Jew. Several Austrians calculated and planned to break the law and lied to authorities all in order to hide the Jewish family. Why would they do this?

The other story is of the man who calculated and planned to dupe investors out of millions, lied to authorities all along and then ended up killing himself … or was it landing in prison. I think I may be getting several well known stories mixed up here. Have you heard of any stories like that?

You see,
GETTING AWAY WITH IT has to do with **what's WRONG** and planning and calculating to so.

ETHICS has to do with **what's right** and planning and calculating to do so.

Just about anything you and I face in our daily lives fall somewhere in between the two stories above, hopefully never as extreme as either. So let's keep them in mind here for the next part of this section on ETHICS.

We have decisions to make. And all during our life we will do things both publicly and privately. I would like to suggest a way for you and I to sleep soundly at night.

VALUE talked about two questions to ask yourself when engaged in any relationship.

This ETHICS section talks about three questions to ask yourself for guidance before any decision. Let's list them here and then briefly consider each:

1-Is it legal and are you sure?
2-Is it honest and are you sure?
3-Honest or not, legal or not, how will folks react if it becomes public knowledge?

The first question deals with some cut and dry, black and white, yes/no ways of thinking. It's actually a two part question. It deals with the law and the defense of yourself should it come into question. Can you point to the laws that are in question and can a lawyer defend your actions? Some people deal with this sort of question multiple times a day and have lawyers and legal departments review everything prior to actions being taken. Some of this may be grayish, but the basis for the question redounds to the law and lawyers and a defense strategy, should it be necessary. Your world may or may not be that intense today. But maybe it is or will be one day.

The second question deals with some gray area for sure and points of view and maybe even differing perspectives. I tend to think of this in terms of a means to an end. Some examples here:

"It depends on what the definition of 'is' is" says a president of the United States being questioned about his actions.

"Read my lips ... " says a president of the United States trying to get elected.

"That expense of new high performance tires? … For my company motorcycle" Says the small business owner working out of his house during an audit with the IRS.

"I will clean it up later" says the teen ager heading out with his/her buddies for the night.

"The company didn't perform well enough this year for bonuses to be more than in prior years," said the small business owner who simply wanted to keep a higher percentage of the profits than had been the practice in prior years. A note here about this person: that was a very good year financially compared to prior years AND the year that followed was the year he lost several of his top employees to the competition. He has had nothing but down years since. But from a certain perspective, he was being honest (question 2) and he didn't break any laws (question 1).

For each of the people in the examples above:
They had a goal in mind.
They steered clear of a direct Legal issue.
They picked an answer that, from a certain perspective, could be considered honest and/or truthful (and from another perspective could be considered a direct and blatant lie).
And finally the means they chose helped them reach their initial goal.

So considering our three questions, the third one may seem a bit provocative. It deals with our convictions to what we know in our heart to be right and wrong. Once we decide to do something and then it becomes publicly known (whether 'public' means our spouse or neighbor or the front page news in our local paper or headline news during primetime), will we feel proud that we did the right thing or embarrassed that we did the wrong thing? Will we be able to look at anyone on our list from the game of "WHO are you?" with a clean conscience and explain why we did it?

The Austrian helpers of Anne Franke's family could very easily explain why what they did was the right thing to do even given that they were committing the highest crime there was in Austria at the time. Question number one for them meant they were breaking the law and they knew it. Question number two meant they would have to lie and scheme and manage the lies for as long they could. They were committing to expending some serious energy to cover their tracks. The last question mattered to them the most here.

The Business guy who duped investors will never have to talk to his three kids about what he did … he killed himself first.

Here is an important note about those three questions: They don't provide an answer and once we can articulate the answer, it doesn't even tell us what to do. We still have to decide what to do once we ask ourselves the questions and come up with our answer. Also notice that these questions don't have a logical follow up question and none of them all alone, or even grouped up as they are here, are adequate for an ethics policy for a company to employ across the executive staff or employees. And however we think about the questions or how we answer them, if we have a faith, we need to consider our teachings there as well and reconcile our actions accordingly. It's a big deal for sure. And it's personal.

I can tell you that there are many executives and professional today who use these simple three questions when it comes to company and business decisions. And they use them personally as well. Some have even changed how they regard their charitable giving and how they spend their personal time and to what degree they find joy in their family life. This stuff is real. Keeping it simple helps it stay real and good. These are just three personal questions that we can let roll around in the back of our head.

Not all of us are faced with extreme situations on a daily basis. But we all face decision making every day that impact others, small and big. The goal is to make the three questions part of that decision process. What's the point? Well, can you think of prior experiences in your life where these three questions, if employed and followed through on by you would have saved you a world of trouble? Can you think of a decision next week that could benefit from reflection using these three questions?

Here's my best guess on where we all stand. This is stuff we already know, and to some degree may already be doing in some way with some self examination with each of our decisions. AND, I will go out on a limb to say that the sort of deliberation each of us do today is already along the lines generally of what these three questions have us consider. The difference is that now that we have seen the questions written, it's now very likely they will be rolling around in the back of our heads for the rest of our life. So how often will we be bold enough to pull them forward during our decision making process? The idea is that if we all know this to be sound thinking, then our goal should be to do it more often and with greater consideration and clarity. That may be a pretty good working title for what it means to have these three questions be 'Top or Mind'.

This is the second secret power, the second bit of magic for the folks I am talking about when I say:

**The happiest, most positively impactful
and personally successful people all
have mastered four things.**

You time again –

Well, here we are at the end of the second section. What did you do last time? Listen to music? Grab a cup of coffee ... skip the little card altogether? All good. Do it again for this one. The next page is another very life like 3"x5" card for you to consider how Ethics will play in your life perhaps a little differently than it did last week.

Again, no pressure. No one sees this stuff. The idea is to think critically about what you really will do with regard to decisions you make, everyday, that will impact you and another person in your life. This can help you start thinking about how those three questions will really fit into your life ... and where ... and with whom.

Check the boxes where it is something where you will consider form now on the questions of Ethics covered in this chapter.

Ethics

Value - **Ethics** - Strengths - True

Considering what ... :

☐ I Say ☐ I do Re:　Work–My time
☐ I Say ☐ I do Re:　Work–What I manage
☐ I Say ☐ I do Re:　Work–My team
☐ I Say ☐ I do Re:　Spouse and/or Family
☐ I Say ☐ I do Re:　Money–earning it
☐ I Say ☐ I do Re:　Money–spending it
☐ I Say ☐ I do Re:　Money–investing it
☐ I Say ☐ I do Re:　Free time/alone time
☐ I Say ☐ I do Re:　_____
☐ I Say ☐ I do Re:　_____
☐ I Say ☐ I do Re:　_____

The point: Considering what you say and what you do in all the important parts of your daily life, ask yourself ...

Is it legal? Am I sure?
And/or
How would I feel if it became known publicly?

© D. Wharram. Top Of Mind. dCoached.com

Strength

I talk with plenty of people that are well aware of 'areas for improvement' in their lives. I have some areas for improvement myself in fact. I actually have plenty of areas for improvement. I ignore some of them. I pay specific attention to other faults I have so that I can work with people, teams or others who can fill the gap. Plus, in some instances I do address them head on working towards some form of improvement. How about you?

I am seeing something pretty cool happen all over the country with business big and small alike. And I like it. The rule of thumb for far too long in the US has been to find areas of improvement and design training and goals to improve those things in people at the place of work.

The trend now however is shifting to find ways to identify STRENGTHS and use those to build the role people will play within the company or on a specific team or assignment. Alignment of goals to strengths is a great new frontier in business. It's a big business and there are some great foundational books on the topic. Look into it some more if you are interested and I encourage it. The topic in this book has us consider a slightly unique slant on the topic and yes, it too may just change your life. But remember - You already know this stuff :-)

I had a personal experience around strengths and weaknesses well before the current trend.

"Where it all started for me as a consultant story"
Very early on in my career I had the responsibility to secure a rehearsal location for a soon to open musical touring England and Europe. Once secured, my job was to prepare the space for the rehearsals. I had a small team to rely on and work with but after about a week, the work to get it ready in the morning and the work to close it up each night became harder and harder for me. Finally all the mistakes I had been making were made known to me in one wonderful encounter with a guy who had been watching closely. I had been given the impression when I rented the place, and so hoping, that this guy was going to get off his butt and lend a hand, but thankfully he was doing something far more important.

The doorman.

I was sweeping the place that night and the doorman came over and asked for the broom. "...finally some help from the guy who I thought was just sitting there all day long." I thought it was odd for him to still be there that late, but I didn't care. I handed him the broom and he asked if I would sit for a moment and he told me that he had some information if I was interested. I just wanted to get out of there for the night, but this seemed interesting. I sat and we chatted. This guy turned out to be a fountain of wisdom to me. I will forever be in debt for what I learned that night.

The way he recounted my shortcomings working with the small team I had was masterful. Masterful because he could articulate the STRENGTHS of each person on my team as well as my own. To be sure he was equally capable to articulate each of our weaknesses as well. He changed my life forever. He walked me back and forth from initial mistakes I had made and their outcomes. He also took the time to explain some possible alternatives that I could have chosen and what those potential outcomes could have looked like instead. It was a lesson focusing on strengths that people around me had and how to make sure everyone was best aligned to where they could provide value to the team, including myself. The way he framed it was such that properly aligned to strengths, our weaknesses had minimum impact, if any, to the work we had in front of us. And we would enjoy the work more. We talked about how to employ some of these changes and what success would and could look like along the way. What we landed on was two very easy measures: 1- people liking their work more than they did today, and 2- A less difficult set of work each morning and each evening.

From that day on till opening night, our team only got better and better, respect among us all grew and true friendships emerged. What a difference. Although this was still work from day to day, it was more along the lines of accomplishing something everyday instead of trudging through it.

A real cool side note to this story: The doorman had

always been 'Jeb' to me. I only learned much later on who he was. He owned the building we were rehearsing in along with three other buildings. Plus, he and his brothers were partners in the production company for whom I had been working to put that show on tour. What a guy. He could have called to have me let go given my initial poor performance. Instead he chose to make who I was … better, based on my strengths.

So let's make this concept personal. Think in terms of things and people around us. When we think of the things or interact with the people, what do we want to see? I like to see nice things and good people. I think everyone does.

In my case, I am a boss, friend, spouse, father, team mate (you have your list too) and in every instance where we interact with the people on our list, we can do so in one of two ways. Do we see the good stuff or the not so good stuff first? Let's meet a couple characters before we think too much more about how we view people.

Imagine if you will, two characters walking down the street. They come across a crabapple tree arching over the sidewalk so much so that they need to duck just a little to get underneath a large branch. The taller of the two says as he looks back over his shoulder,

"Someone must be taking good care of that tree for it to be so healthy and full of fruit. That's not easy when we have a hot summer like we are having."

Shorty says, "I have always found the fruit too sour for anything no matter how it's prepared. And I would trim it back this fall so it doesn't have the overhang next summer."

The two continue on and come upon a window display for a cake shop. Again the taller of the two is the first to comment,

"Look at the frosting there on that cake. Imagine the expertise someone has to have to be so perfect. When I try and frost a cake for my kids it's usually something of a disaster that we all have a good laugh over." He smiles thinking of the last time this occurred in his home.

The short guy smiles of course, it is a cute little glimpse into the tall guys life, "I agree. How did they accidentally get frosting down there in the corner of the window I wonder? I would clean the outside of the window as well and dress it up a bit if it were my shop."

The two continue on again and come to a lonely little fire hydrant where the tall guy prompts them to stop.

"I've grown up in this town and I remember this fire hydrant from when I was a kid. Think of all the kids and all the hot summer days when they opened it for us to play and cool off. Great memories!"

"I can't imagine how many dogs have visited it over the years. Yuck. I would move everyone to the park right over there if I saw them playing here today," answered the short fella staring at the nice playground.

Introducing these characters is not about the Optimist vs. the Pessimist or even the old adage "… silver lining in every cloud." I am pointing out the habits in our everyday approach. It's how we see things and how we interact everyday. The story is my long winded way of pointing out something that can be said quite bluntly:

We all have strengths and weaknesses. The expert tree keeper may have overlooked the needed pruning. The master cake maker smeared some frosting and the store keeper who has such talent on staff overlooked a dirty window. The tall guy sees all the fun despite a sanitary issue with the hydrant. BUT, when we interact with someone, which do we hope they focus on first? I can tell you that as an employee, if you want to ruin my day start by telling me something bad about me. As an employer, I know that people who smile first because they are recognized for an achievement have a more productive day or week or month.

So when called upon to tend to a tree, frost a cake, supervise kids playing on a hot day by a hydrant-

The tall fella will know **who** to ask for advice on tending a tree, **who** to call upon to for their expertise frosting a cake and will laugh **along with** the kids at the open hydrant. He sees the big picture to start and builds from there.

The short friend will know what **he would do** to keep the tree trimmed back off the sidewalk, what **he would do** to dress up a window and **what he would NOT** have the kids play next to. He sees the issues first.

Both are valid but one starts with the strengths right in front of him and builds from there. The other thinks of what opinions he has and will exhaust that first to get the project moving. One knows who else needs to be involved. The other knows what he would do first.

I can think of bosses and managers and owners and CEO's as well as moms and dads and brothers and sisters and friends in both camps. You can too, probably. You probably identified yourself with one of the two and made a few adjustments to make it fit you a little closer. Maybe a blend of the two are a good description of you? There are two points to this example.

To be clear, not one of them is preferred or better than the other. The first point is to put an emphasis on strengths that may not be part of our current thinking when looking at people with whom we work, live and play. And if we already think of strengths first, then consider this a reinforcement or clarifier for any of us. It's a good thing. Only good things come from recognizing strengths.

The second point needs a little bit of a story to help make clear.

For some of my friends and colleagues who stop by my office, I have toys and trinkets and things to play with or look at on my desk. One of my favorites is a 'gazing block'. (*And as a side note … if I ever work personally with you or your team(s), act surprised when I bring up the gazing block for a discussion on this topic.)* Anyway, it is a cubed block of wood I made inspired by the whimsical movie, 'Mr. Magorium's Wonder Emporium' starring Dustin Hoffman. Mr. Magorium owns and freely shares a mysterious magic wood block. I won't give away the movie. My version of the wooden cube is for gazing at and considering what you see. My block is magic, of course, like Mr. Magorium's, but a different kind of magic for everyone. Some will see something really cool, some will see things that may be at odds with other elements they see. Others will see those same elements and consider it artistic or technically interesting. Still others will see the flaws and mistakes because they do exist both naturally and because of my workmanship in certain ways. Again there is nothing wrong with any perception but I can tell you one thing that is pretty consistent from my point of view. Whether or not the person gazing at the block has a hobby including wood work, metal work, arts and crafts, or is an artist or artisan, sculptor, is old or young, the most fascinating people will make an immediate assumption that I made it and a follow-up question as to why I made it or how I started the process. And frankly, the least fascinating individuals are those that see the flaws first with answers as to how they would have done it differently to avoid it. Flaws are by far the most visible thing to see and are always the top candidates for what we would improve upon next time. They are very important to note for sure and learn from potentially for future reference or even work to correct perhaps. So the second point is to be careful about the weight given and the timing of considering any solutions around flaws and shortcomings. Rarely are those the things, and nearly never is that the stuff that will be the foundational building blocks of any person, project, event or relationship.

Strengths are something special that people know are in them someplace. Good people have strengths and want to employ them.
Great people bring out those strengths in others.

Is a focus on STRENGTHS really worth it? Making something better has tremendous value, doesn't it?

Over the years I have learned three things along the topic of strengths and these perceptions will lead us into the slightly unique slant on the topic I promised.

One thing:
Think of your list from the game of 'Who are you?' I know that as a father, boss and team member, when I start out defining individuals by their strengths, defining goals and setting expectations based on their strengths, THEY are far more driven to exceed, enjoy their work, have stronger and better relationships professionally and they respect me in our relationship. A couple nice side effects occur as well. Finding a way to offset any weaknesses or shortcomings is a joint effort and far more successfully bought into by all. And secondly, the atmosphere is one that is far more resilient to any setbacks and far more responsive to any opportunity. In short, we are more suited for what is in front of us no matter what that may be when we are allowed to face it from a point of strength versus one of weakness.

The second thing:
Looking back over my career where I worked for someone who considered my strengths first … I'm talking about bosses I have had over the years, I liked those jobs best and money had nothing to do with it.

Some real quick examples:
Paper boy first with my brother. He called me a wimp because I could not throw the paper as far as he could. I didn't like that boss, but I liked the job so I found another boss.

Paper boy helper with my friend. He could throw way further than I (just like my brother could) but I could peddle the bike with the load of our papers. As a team, I peddled with the full load and he walked throwing papers as we went. It was awesome. It could have been that way for me and my brother but hey, I was a wimp and that's as far as we explored our abilities to work together.

Busboy for a family restaurant. I wasn't family and it showed. They were nice to me, maybe hired me to be helpful to my family but I was an outsider. That's an awful way to be defined.

Caddy. I had a great set of clients for three summers. These two fellas considered me and the other caddy as part of their team. They asked us about which clubs to use and where we thought they should play certain fairways or greens. Because I loved being part of the team, I went a few extra steps to clean my guy's clubs and bag after every round before putting them back in his locker at the clubhouse. Now the other caddy just saw this as a good tipping gig and focused on the money alone (they really tipped us very well … we were the envy of the caddy shack). My second and third year with these two guys - I double-caddied and the other caddy was out. And for two years (all year long) I worked for their two families personally apart from the golf course. When I look back, the best and strongest relationships are a two-way street that starts by expecting the best from each other and never swaying from that. If it's not your thing, you can go somewhere else. The other caddy did and we stayed friends as well.

Busboy and Cook in high school. Mr. B owned the joint and three of us friends started as busboys at the same time. Over the course of the first half of the year or so, Mr. B watched us and then met with each of us separately. He wanted to see me in the kitchen within 6 months as a head cook. He wanted to see the other as a main room host within six months and the third fella was a hard worker, but Mr. B helped him get a job as a mechanics helper at the body shop not far away. When I look back at what he did, he considered how I interacted with the cooks and everyone in the kitchen to see how that all worked. It was an interest to me and every so often they would put me on the grill to see if I could make pancakes and they taught me a few things about making the rest of the food on the menu. The other fella always showed up in a slacks and a nice shirt and chatted first with the host on duty and maybe a few customers as they came or went and he was good at it. The last guy was a car and motorcycle guy always talking about and working on his car and motorbike, sometimes, even in the parking lot of the restaurant. Mr. B aligned us to our strengths. He had to have. He had to see things in each of us and ask himself how he could move us in a direction more aligned to where we had shown promise and what he had to offer. I loved that place. I worked there four years and was the head cook for more than two of those years before heading off to college.

Finally … the third thing

Remember that theme of sorts we keep revisiting?

> **The happiest, most positively impactful
> and personally successful people all
> have mastered four things.**

The folks that theme above describes have mastered seeing strengths first in people. That's their secret sauce.

They simply find themselves caring more about learning what makes people tick and what makes them great and then employs it however they can.

I have one executive friend that I know for a fact hates wasting time. He has told me that exactly, "I hate anything that wastes time". He's pretty clear about it. He is driven like you wouldn't believe and it really is of no surprise that he will not tolerate spending time where it is not valuably spent according to him. Do you know where I see him mostly? Talking to people about their lives. He's a business guy that runs a multimillion dollar data company. He spends his time talking to people in his halls about fishing, hunting, cars, boats, their kids, college, sports, cooking … everything that is of personal interest to those with whom he is talking. He must find that valuable time. Time learning what is of interest to others in his company. I know he mixes that knowledge he learns of these people with his interactions with them professionally to make sure they stay focused on the things that are important. I know he uses it as a guide to make sure that the work people are doing doesn't depress them or hold them back and he can tell if there is a dramatic shift in things happening personally with other interests. He can help adjust things at work if it's having a negative impact on their personal lives. He's mastered a few things. Four things actually … we've talked about three of them so far.

Each of us can harness this kind of focus for the rest of our life — starting next week, or tomorrow … or even our very next encounter with another live human being.

~~~

So far:

VALUE talked about two questions to ask yourself when engaged in any relationship.

ETHICS section talks about three questions to ask yourself for guidance before any decision.

Now add this:
STRENGTH has only one question … well maybe two:

> **What strengths define the person
> (group/team etc.) right in front of us?**
>
> And maybe we want also ask:
> **What am I focusing on first?**

That second potential question is more about our perspective in starting something up, like a project, getting a team together, planning something new or renewing something that isn't going quite right.

I know there are plenty of books on Strengths and management styles and looking for the best things in people and self. This is all AWESOME stuff but the caution is to not over-complicate this topic. Learn all that stuff, of course, if you are interested. Read the books for pointers and refinements, but don't lose perspective.

We already know what is good and what is bad. Someone taught it to, or demonstrated it for us when we were very young. In my case, I think of my grampa. Who do you think of? We know how that knowledge already inside our head of what is good and what is bad applies to business, family, relationships, friends etc. We all know positive and good things about the people we see, work with, live with and interact with everyday. Keeping it as simple as asking ourselves what we are going to see first and what we use to define the people right in front of us will, absolutely will, impact us, THEM and the RELATIONSHIP from that point forward.

We are in control of that regardless of where they are in their world and how they regard us. If it's a problem for someone in your world, give them this book and include a book mark for the section you think they might enjoy most.

Given all the people out there in the world, the best of the best folks I know look at strengths first in people even if the person to whom they are looking doesn't see it in themselves. The best of the best out there never get discouraged helping someone else realize their true strengths. And the best of the best out there look for the simplest route to get those strengths employed/recognized/honed etc. It's that simple. And it's that consistent. Whether it's just part of their DNA or part of their deliberation, they ALWAYS answer the question: "What defines the people right in front of you?" - Strengths!

This is the third secret power, the third bit of magic for the folks I am talking about when I say:

The happiest, most positively impactful and personally successful people all have mastered four things.

Ok ... you know the drill here but this time you have to do all the work. In the first blank enter some real names of real people in your life. Fill in the blank right next to it with a strength you know exists with that person. There are two sections each with its own slant.

Strength

Value - Ethics - **Strength** - True

Who do you expect to run into in the next 7 days? And what strength will you see first?

☐ _____ _____

☐ _____ _____

☐ _____ _____

☐ _____ _____

☐ _____ _____

Who will you seek out in the next 7 days to redefine which strengths you see in them?

☐ _____ _____

☐ _____ _____

☐ _____ _____

☐ _____ _____

☐ _____ _____

The point: When interacting with others, what defines them is key. Ask yourself ...

What strengths define the person (group/team etc.) right in front of us?
And maybe we want also ask:
What am I focusing on first?

© D. Wharram. Top Of Mind. dCoached.com

I am going to add a little bit to the recap here:

VALUE talked about two questions. The idea focused on the **relationship** we have with all the people in our life.

ETHICS talked about three questions. The idea focused personally on **ourselves** and the choices we make as well as why and how we make them.

STRENGTH talked about one, or maybe two questions. The idea focused on the defining qualities of **all the people** with whom we interact.

Let's keep all those in mind as we think through what it means to be TRUE.

Initially, when we think of the word TRUE we may think about it in terms of being the opposite of false. Or maybe we think of it in terms of telling the truth, the whole truth, etc.

In fact, this bucket of information falls under another meaning for the word. Let's think about True as in real, in-tune and genuine. Think about it in terms of a building perhaps. An architect designs buildings to be True to parallel and perpendicular for the weight bearing to be longstanding. My grandfather was a watchmaker and the best hand-made watches in the world are true to the measure of time, making their value extreme. True has everything to do with being the real thing ... not a fake, not a knock off, not a pretender.

I have worked with people who have journeyed in earnest into the pits of hell by allowing who they truly were to be sidetracked by so many things. The truth of the matter is, that who they truly WERE changed and who they truly BECAME was a very sad reality based on some things that started as something small but were awful and had no bounds. Things that if they had considered their Value, their Ethics, the Strengths of those around them, they would have stopped short of diving headlong through those fiery gates. I have also had the good fortune to work with some of the best and brightest minds in business and other walks of life that demonstrated how their convictions ultimately play into the success of their business, teams, families or themselves as a person. These are the experiences from which I am drawing when it comes to how this book considered what it means to be TRUE.

It does in fact boil down to being genuine. That's the basis for who the TRUE you really is. Thinking again of those individuals across my career and life (and probably yours too):

**The happiest, most positively impactful
and personally successful people all
have mastered four things.**

The common denominator is that who they are is based on how Value, Ethics and Strengths are just part of who they genuinely are.

Taking this to the personal level here:

Are we aware and consistent in resolving to provide VALUE to every interaction?

Do we regard our ETHICS with sound decision making every time we are committing to anything, especially when it impacts others?

Do we define the folks right in front of us based on their STRENGTHS?

And do we think about these things naturally and without any pretenses? This is ultimately how we are defined. Consider if someone took the time to document on paper all the ways in which we could be defined. Would anyone with whom we interact be surprised with what they would read? Would they see things on that page that were not honest perhaps from their knowledge of how they know you? Would they see something that is a complete foreign concept to them regarding how you fit into their lives? Would something they know about you seem missing from the list somehow? And would that missing thing they would or could share about you be good or bad? To whom? And are you OK with that?

Let's be cautious for a moment about what that can mean. For instance, my mother-in-law is in her 80's and wants to parachute or skydive once. Now when she said that out loud to all of us, it surprised and delighted us to know this at the same time. What a fun and exciting side to her that we all get to learn. We were surprised and it only added in a positive way to our understanding of who she truly is. Now I can tell you that if she were to tell us that she secretly embezzled a million dollars from some place, that too would surprise us but for very different reasons. And I am pretty sure our understanding of who she truly is would forever be changed and not in a good way.

Consider some of the high profile things around famous people or business icons where we learn some ugly dark secret they have covered up elaborately over the years and it surprised us. These things change how we regard them for sure. In some instances, perhaps that regard cannot be redeemed. Maybe it can, but the fundamental understanding of who they were and who they are to us now is different and the stability of that regard has been diminished. We are developing a full and complete picture of who they really are.

How about the Politician that said one thing and did the opposite? In that case, we may not be surprised, just angry because we were so hoping for what they said to be the case. Not surprising, but this is how we start to hone in on which candidates we will support and those who we will not. It is also the foundation of how much importance people have in our lives as well as how we understand the importance of our lives to others.

And how about the person in front of you at the drive-through who you do not know and will likely never meet, that pays your bill for you. It's an act from someone that impacts your life and what you do with that will (or will not) impact others. Will the change in your life be a surprise to others in your life? Will it be a good surprise or bad?

~~~

The secret to keeping our TRUE self in check:

It's the point of this book. It's a small grouping of questions on four topics that we now can put in the back of our head to be sure the best parts of what we know to be good stay Top of Mind.

VALUE … Resolve to provide it with two questions to yourself with each and every interaction:

>If we are the first one to talk, the question to ask ourselves in our head,
>### **"How can I help?"**

>If we are listening first, the question to ask ourselves in our head:
>### **"What can I learn?"**

ETHICS ... This is a personal matter for each of us.

> **1-Is it legal and are you sure?**
> **2-Is it honest and are you sure?**
> **3-Honest or not, legal or not, how will folks react if it becomes public knowledge?**

Strength ... This is in regard to all the people in our life.

> **What strengths define the person (group/team etc.) right in front of us?**
>
> And maybe we want also ask:
> **What am I focusing on first?**

Now as we go about our life doing things, making decisions, interacting with people, groups, teams, friends and family and as we live life and others see us living it, for **True,** we need to ask ourselves one simple question:

> **Who will this surprise? And why?**
>
> Then, put on our Good/bad hat and see if how we are defined changes ... and is that kind of surprise OK?

This is one of those questions that maybe we need to think about to start our day before we head out to deal with the things we have planned. And maybe it's one of those questions we have to ask ourselves in hindsight at the end of the day regarding those things we did that weren't part of our plans heading into the day.

To tie all of this together, for me, it seems I grasp things better if I can recognize telltale signs that things are NOT working out and that my TRUE SELF is falling apart. See if any of these notes resonate with you to wrap it up:

VALUE is all about resolving to provide it at every turn where each of us and someone else is involved. The TRUE you falls apart when the value we bring means listening just enough to know how best to display ourselves to impress. We are not actually paying attention with the intent to learn anything, and we don't focus on what we can do to help. We are just preparing how to respond and sound and/or look great when it's our turn.

ETHICS is about being sound in our decision-making so we can sleep well at night for all the right reasons. The TRUE you falls apart when the base for our ethics is only as far reaching as finding the rationalization to do it, what ever 'it' is.

STRENGTH is about seeing the best in people and defining them based on that as a starting point from which to build. The TRUE you falls apart when we look for those attributes (strengths or shortcomings) that can be manipulated to our purposes alone. Or worse still, we skip considering the strengths people have and focus on their failures, flaws and weaknesses and define them starting there.

TRUE is about who we are, not necessarily our

character. True is not whether we are introvert or extravert or our style, accent or type of watch we wear or about being humorous or not. The TRUE you falls apart when we are mostly in the business of impressing people. The TRUE self is instead generally impressed by the people, teams and others around him/her.

~~~

One last one for you to think about:

True

Value - Ethics - Strengths - **True**

In the blanks, inventory words, actions, characteristics, secrets, whatever that could be used to describe you ... Then take the time to consider if it is how you could be known among your friends, family and professionally.

Known by those at work:

_____ Would surprise ☐ Family ☐ Friends

_____ Would surprise ☐ Family ☐ Friends

_____ Would surprise ☐ Family ☐ Friends

Known by my family:

_____ Would surprise ☐ Work ☐ Friends

_____ Would surprise ☐ Work ☐ Friends

_____ Would surprise ☐ Work ☐ Friends

Known by my Friends:

_____ Would surprise ☐ Work ☐ Family

_____ Would surprise ☐ Work ☐ Family

_____ Would surprise ☐ Work ☐ Family

Who will this surprise? And why?

Then, put your Good/bad hat on and see if how you are defined changes. Is that all OK with you?

© D. Wharram. Top Of Mind. dCoached.com

Follow up?

The happiest, most positively impactful and personally successful people all have mastered four things.

Regarding <u>Relationships</u> - We are talking about the important stuff when it comes to our impact on others and how we listen and engage with them in a relationship (**Value**).

Regarding <u>Self</u> - We are talking about the surety in our decisions, well aware of the impact our decisions have on others and our ability to deal with that openly and with a clear conscience (**Ethics**).

Regarding <u>Others</u> - We are talking about seeing first, perhaps seeking out first, the best parts of anyone with whom we interact (**Strength**).

The **TRUE** you is best understood when whatever we do, whatever anyone says about us, nothing will surprise anyone else in our life. And if it does, will that have a positive or negative impact on who we are in any relationship? In short, The True you is about the impact of our life and being aware of it.

At the end of each section there was a little one page activity where you had the opportunity to reflect on the topic. I do hope you took advantage of the exercise, and again, I want to emphasize that you don't need to share that stuff with anyone. That's personal … and it's all about you.

In my experience, most people don't like doing workbooks in settings with others (some, of course, do but most don't), and rarely do we write in paperback books the way I have asked you to here. So we find ourselves perhaps at an awkward place in the book.

You see, in a group setting at this point, everyone is holding four 3"x5" cards and some may have checkmarks and things written down on them. Everyone is wondering if I am going to call for volunteers to share what they have written or what they have checked off. I don't do that. That's not cool. If we did this right, the things you marked off on those sheets is very personal and have meaning only to you. So let's keep it that way.

But what you can do is add up all the check boxes you checked and record that number on the next page.

If you want to share that number with me, GREAT!
This whole book is based on a half day workshop, and the exercise at the end of each section is what I call "Putting on the VEST". It's a time where we take some very simple notes after reflection on how this will all be part of our lives next week.

Those of you that fill out the last page of this book and

share that number with me will also be the group of folks that get a copy of the follow on book in Draft/Review digital form.

That book is going to include some statistics around the numbers people land on, some Questions and Answers that I have addressed over the years … and new questions that people will send me along with their numbers.

The last page has a couple more details … and I do look forward to hearing from you!

-- Send me an email --

1. Count all the checkboxes you checked in the other four cards.
2. *Enter the number in this box:*

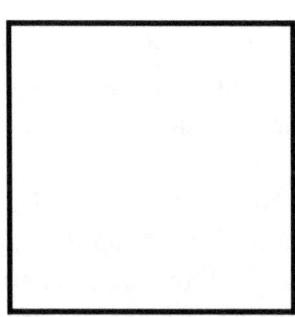

Send me a note with two things:
- domwharram@gmail.com
- VEST in the subject line
- Your name and the number you entered in that box above

You will receive 2 emails from me *(and I actually don't do anything else with your email at all)*:
-   **One in 1 week**, to remind you of this number and the importance of it in your life.

-   **One in 2 months** to ask you for your feedback about the value of this information in your life.

When you send me your number and name, feel free to include any questions you may have for the follow-up Q&A book.

ABOUT THE AUTHOR

Over the past twenty-five years, Dom has been an Executive Consultant, Change Agent, Author & Entrepreneur in multiple industries.

Dom serves at the request of CEO's and board's, working with small leadership teams and individual executives as an architect, coach and evangelist for complex programs and transformational initiatives. He focuses on collaborate organizational development for team and leadership success.

Dom has three children and lives with his wife in Minnesota where he can be found in his wood shop most of his free time.

You can learn more by visiting:

www.dCoached.com